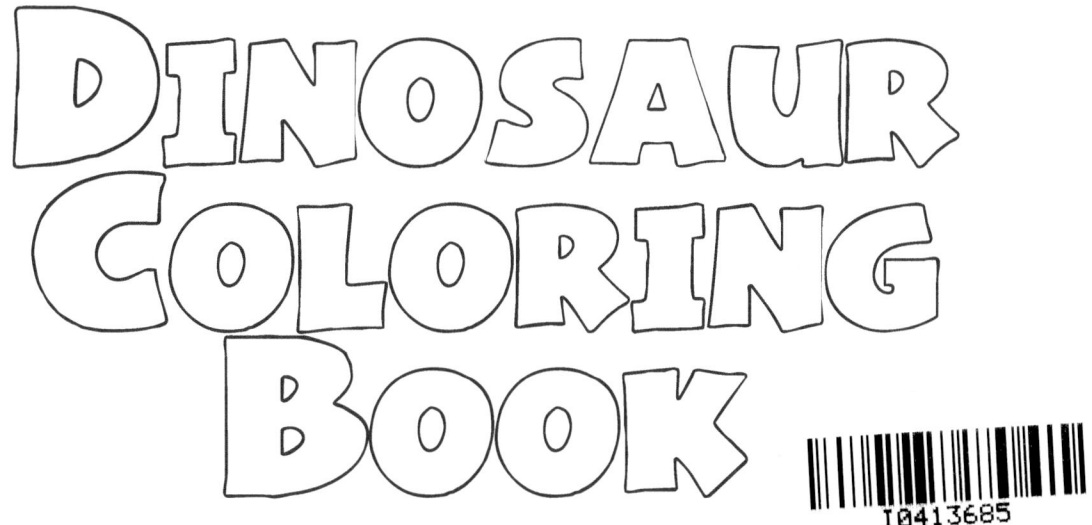

DINOSAUR COLORING BOOK

BY SUSAN POTTERFIELDS

ISBN: 10: 1534838457
ISBN-13:978-1534838451

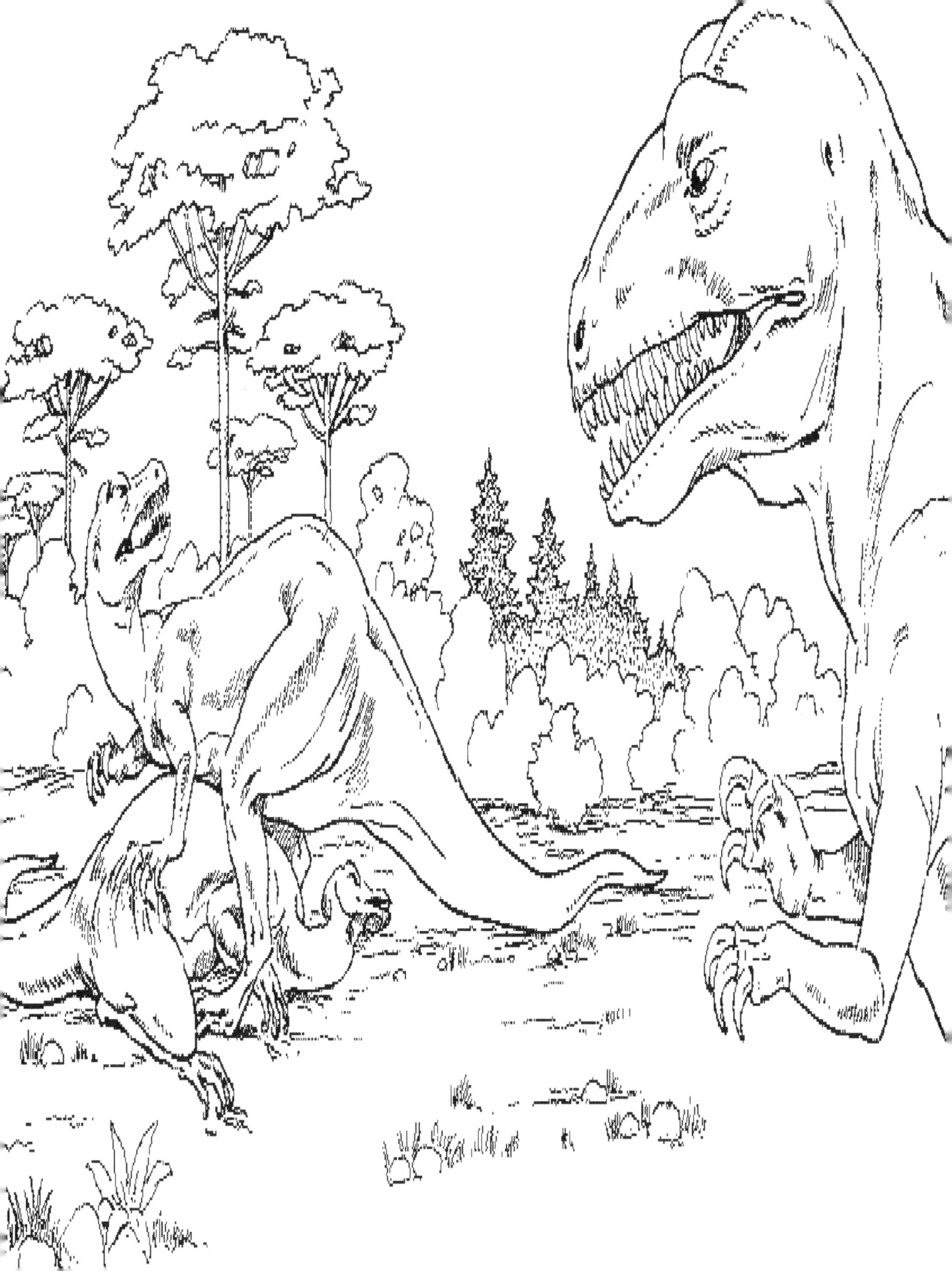

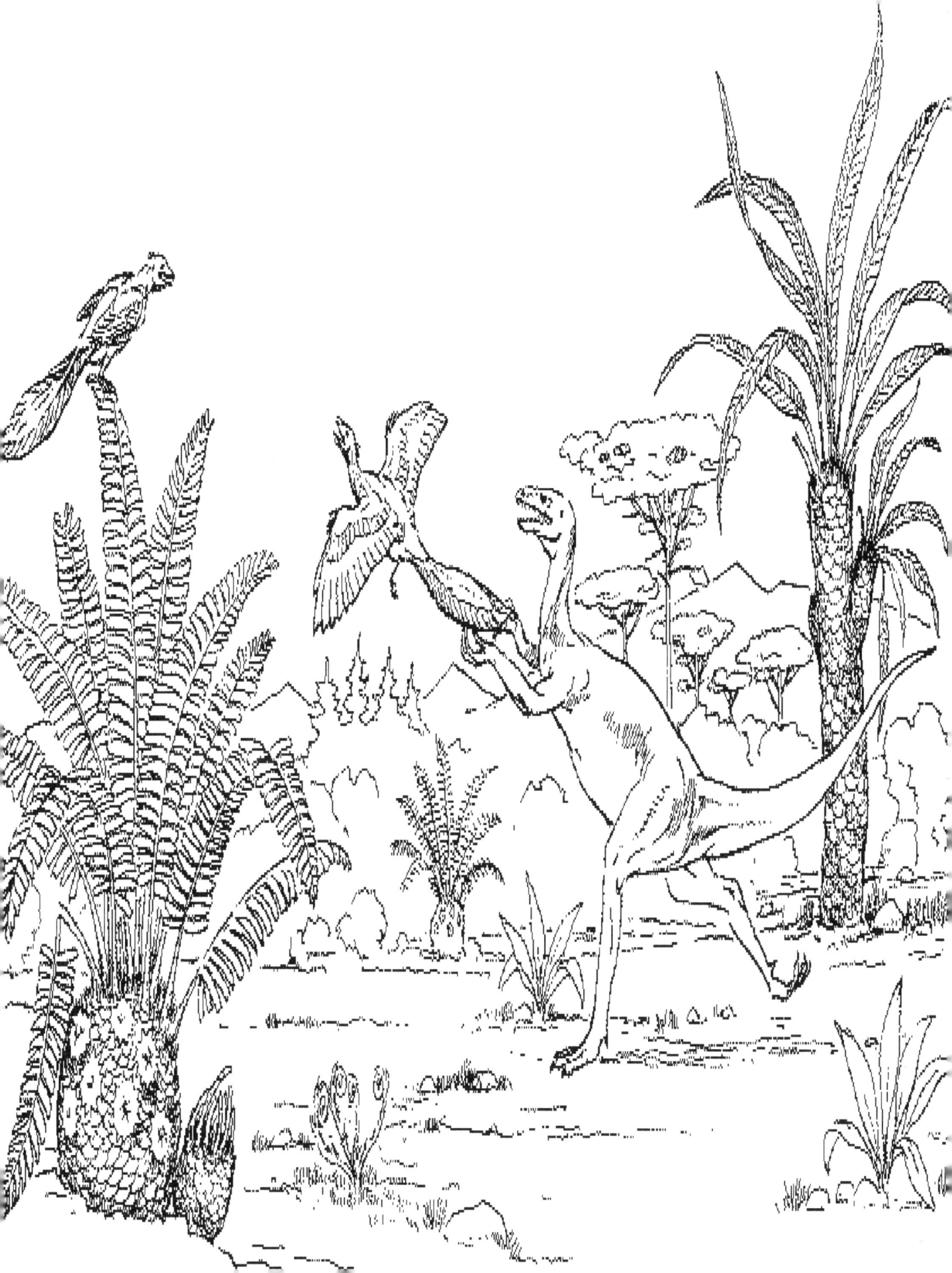

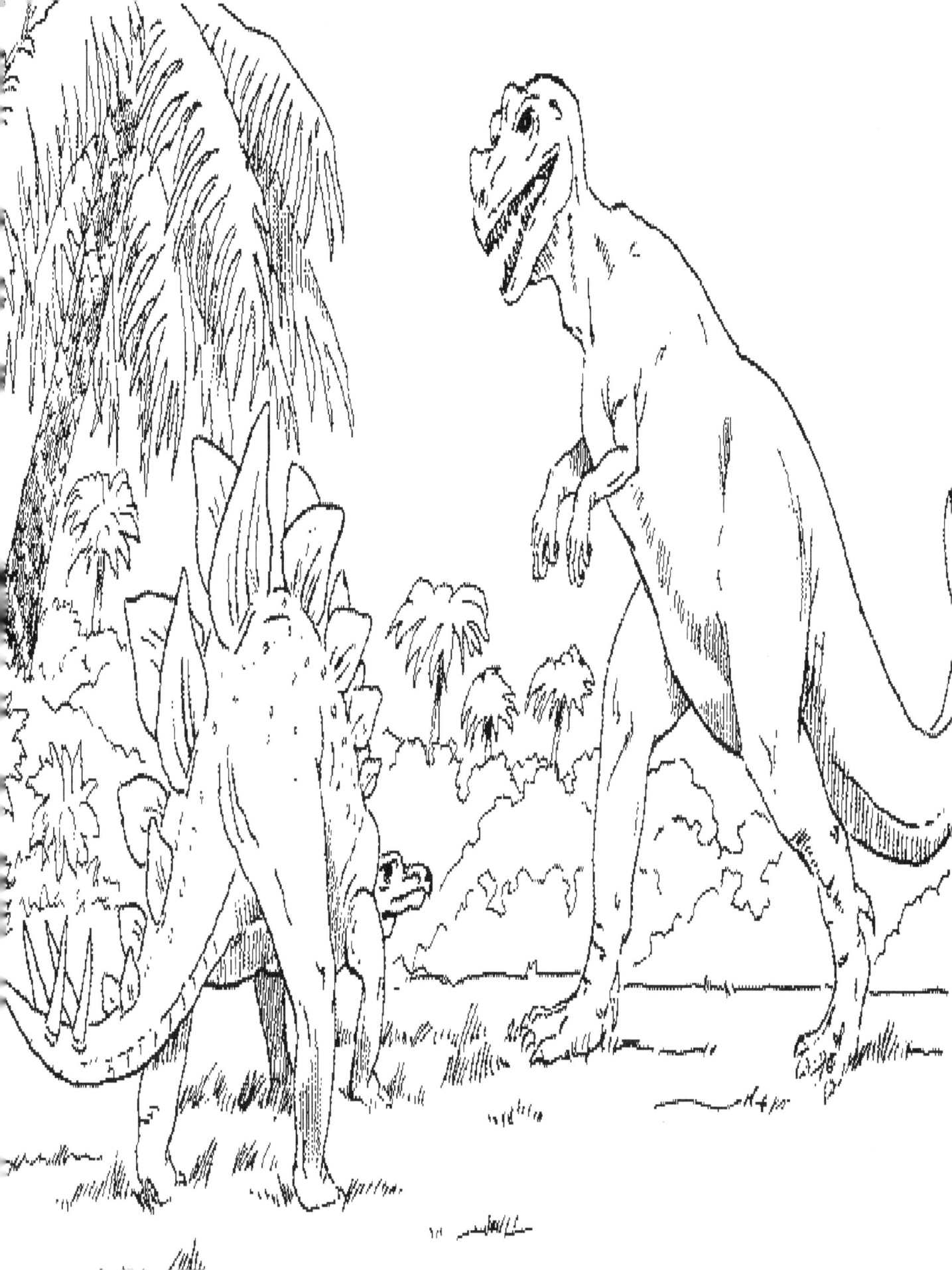

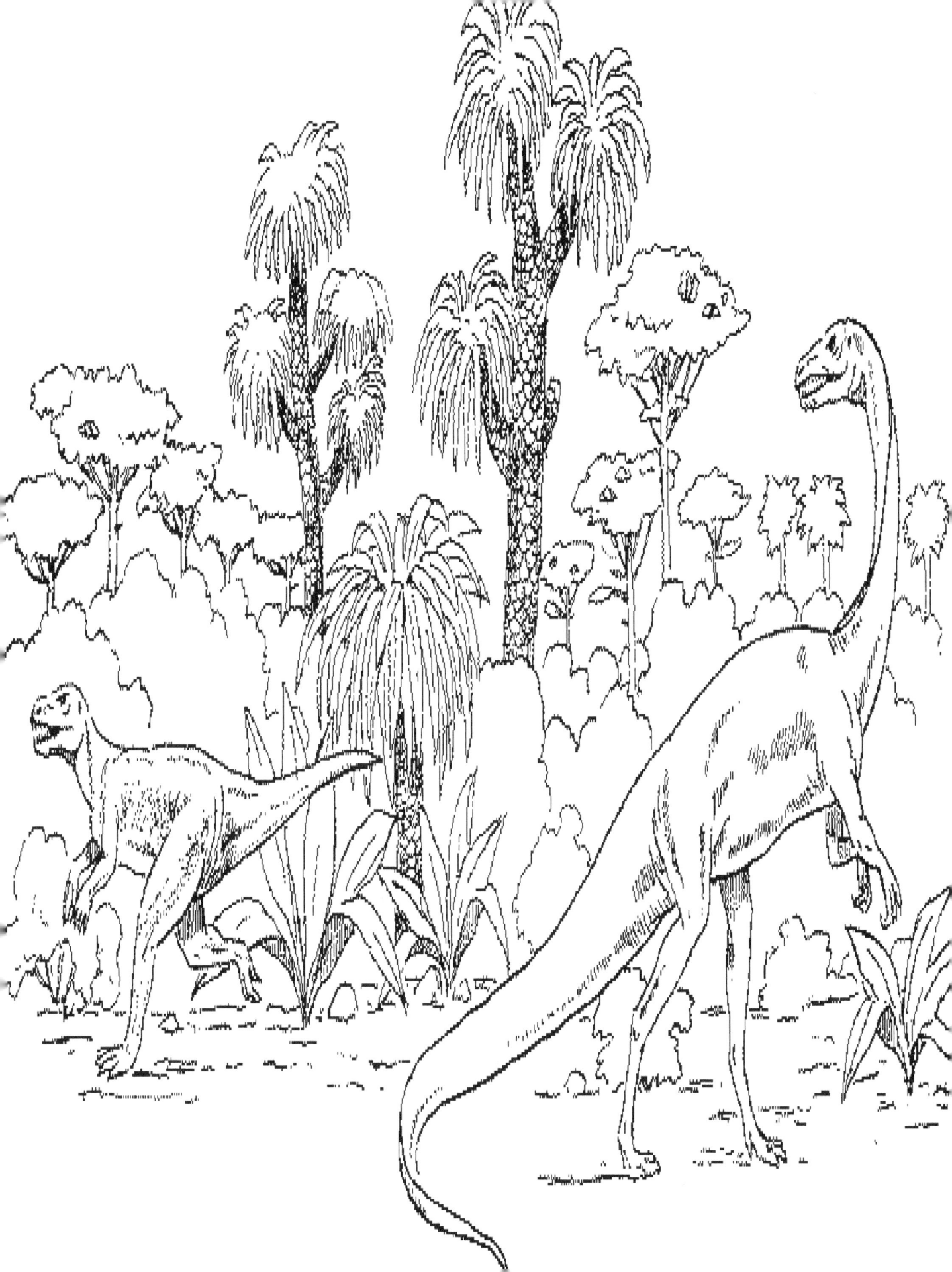

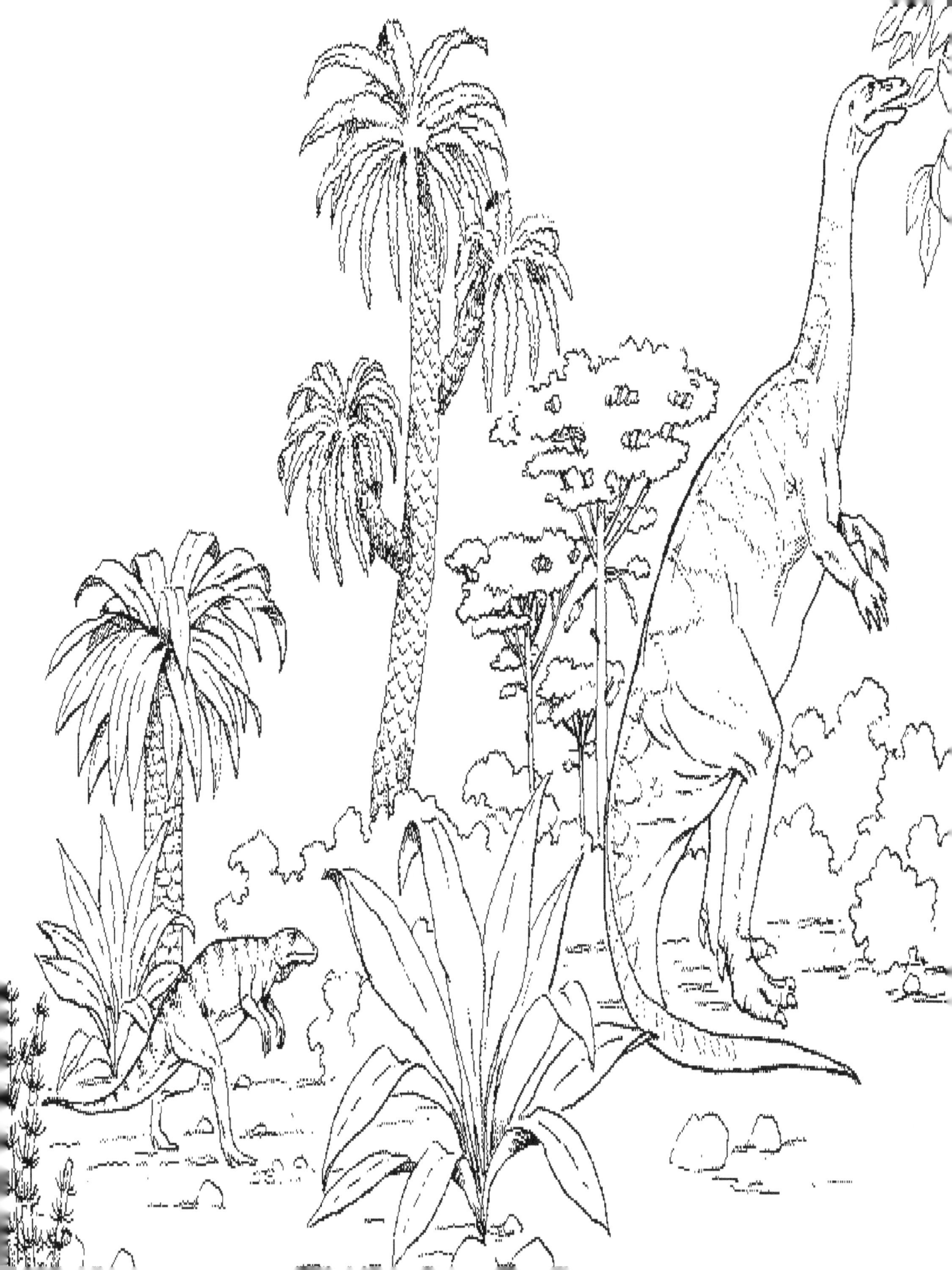

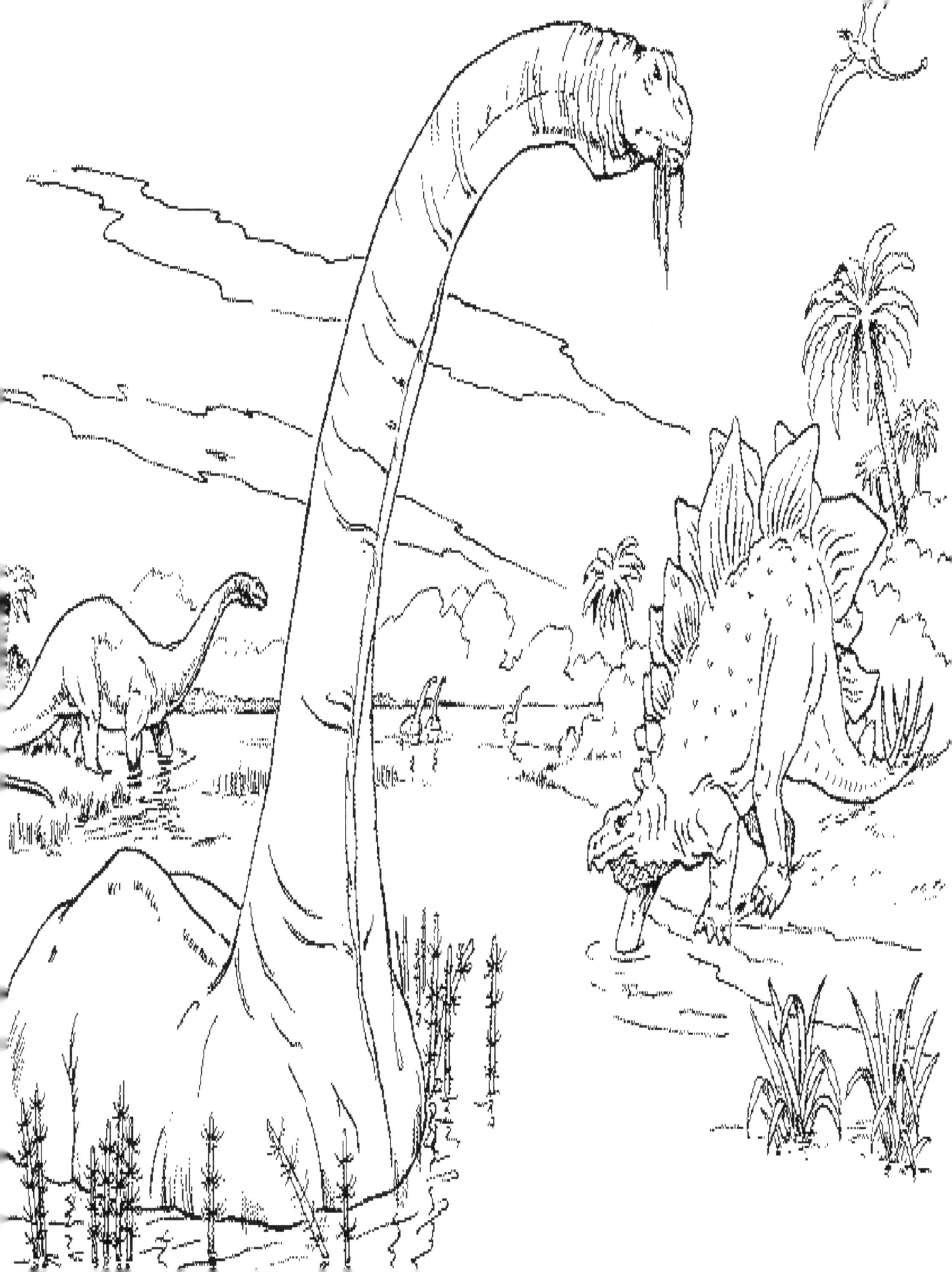

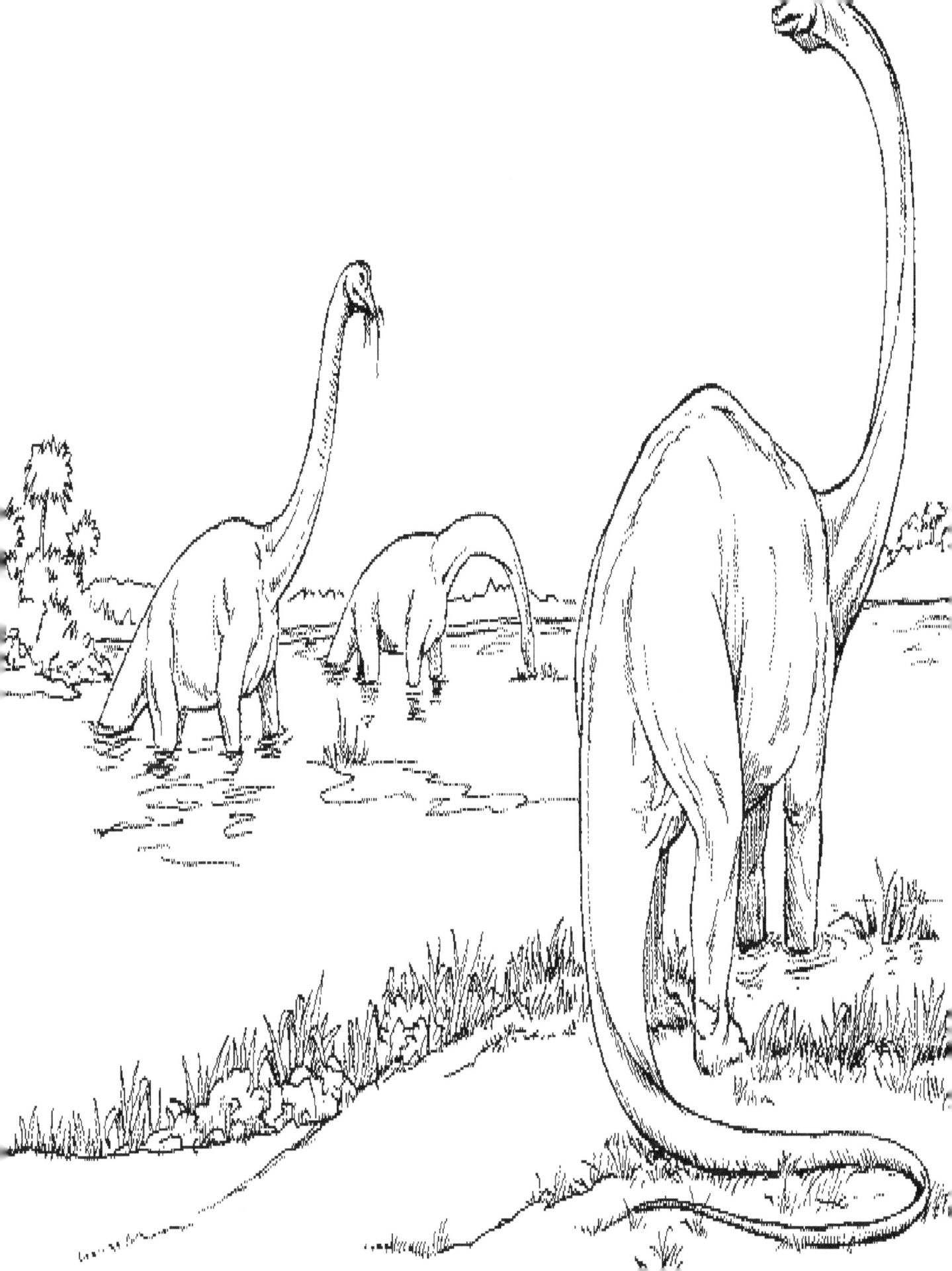

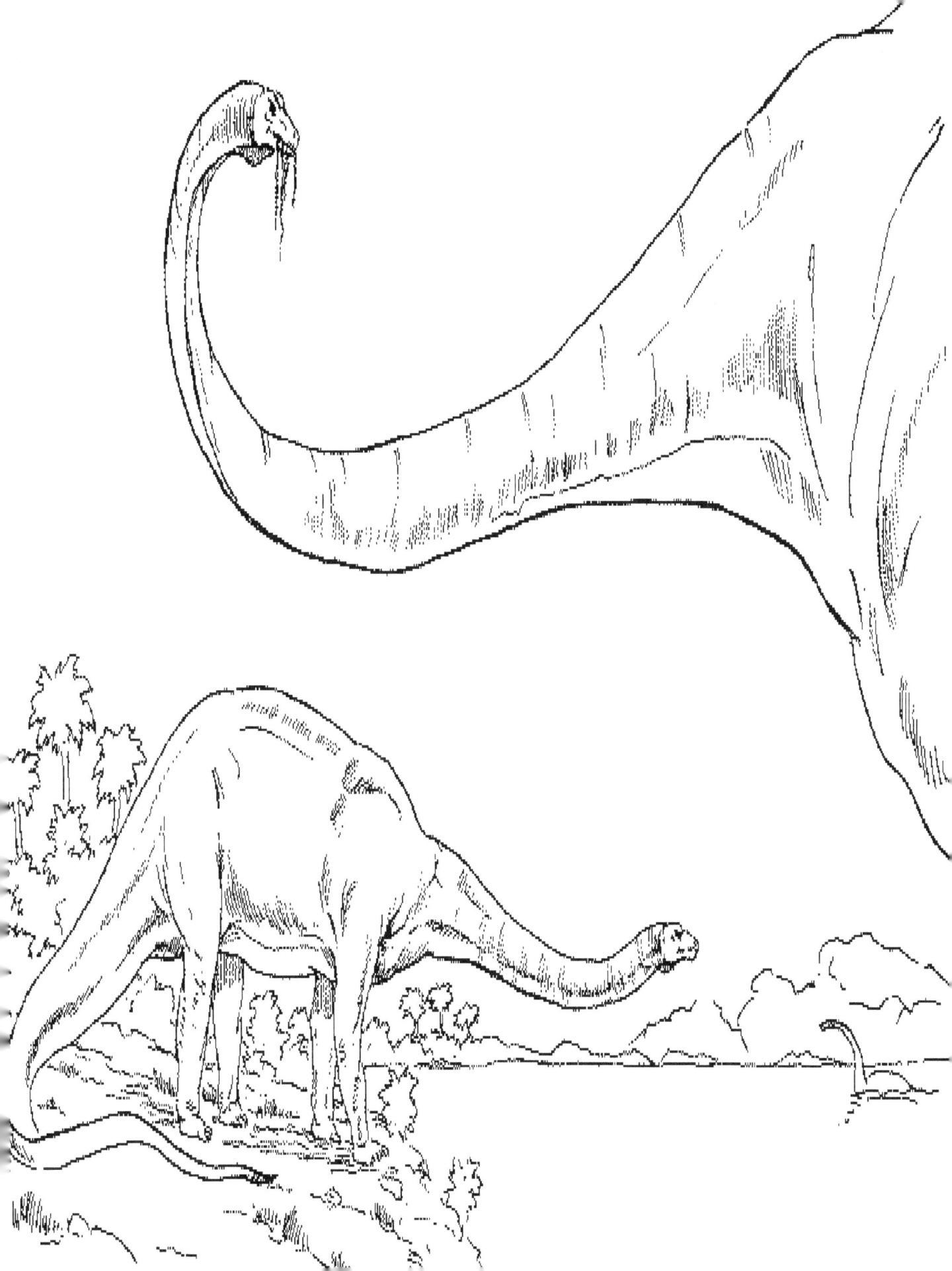

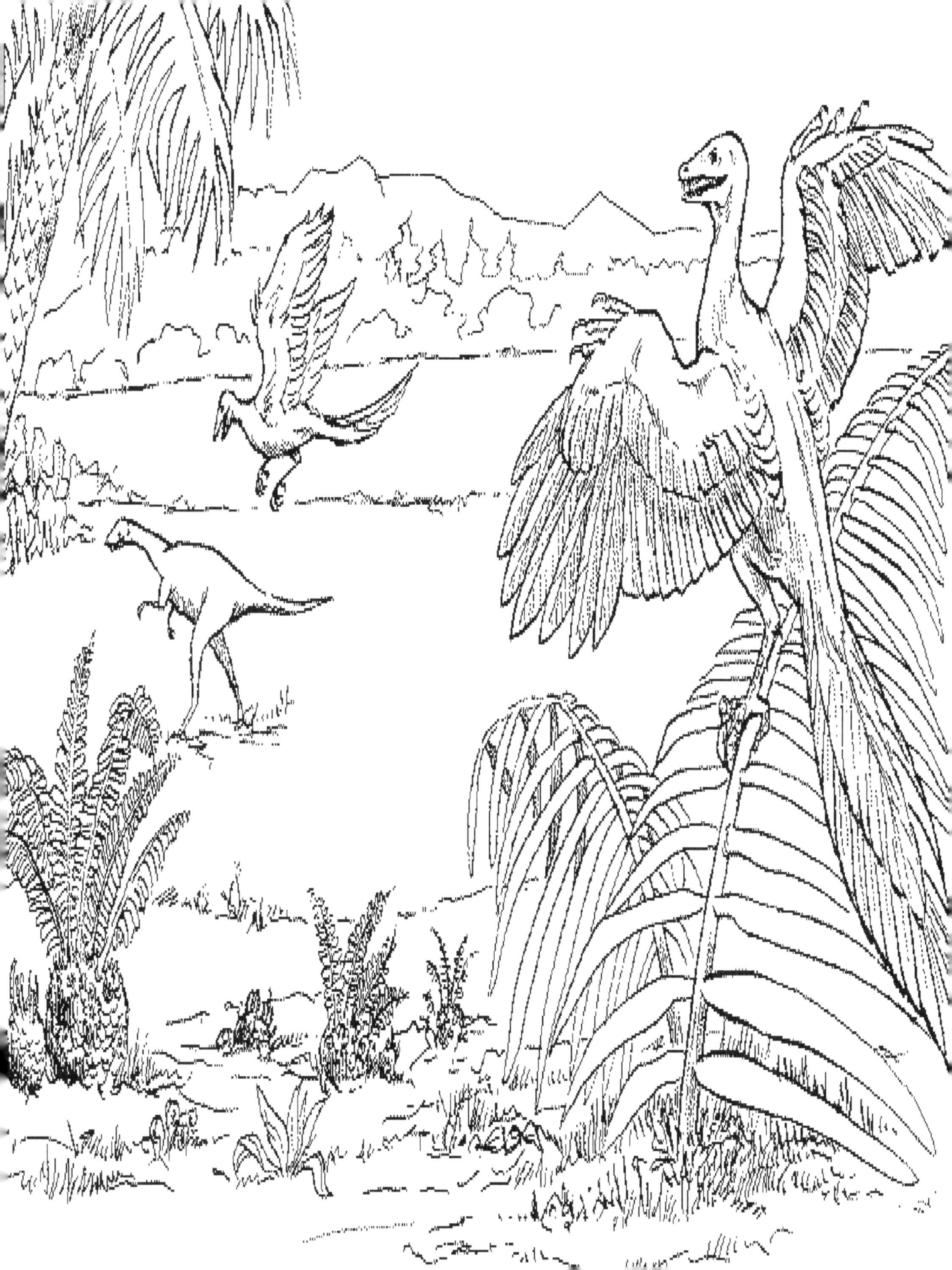

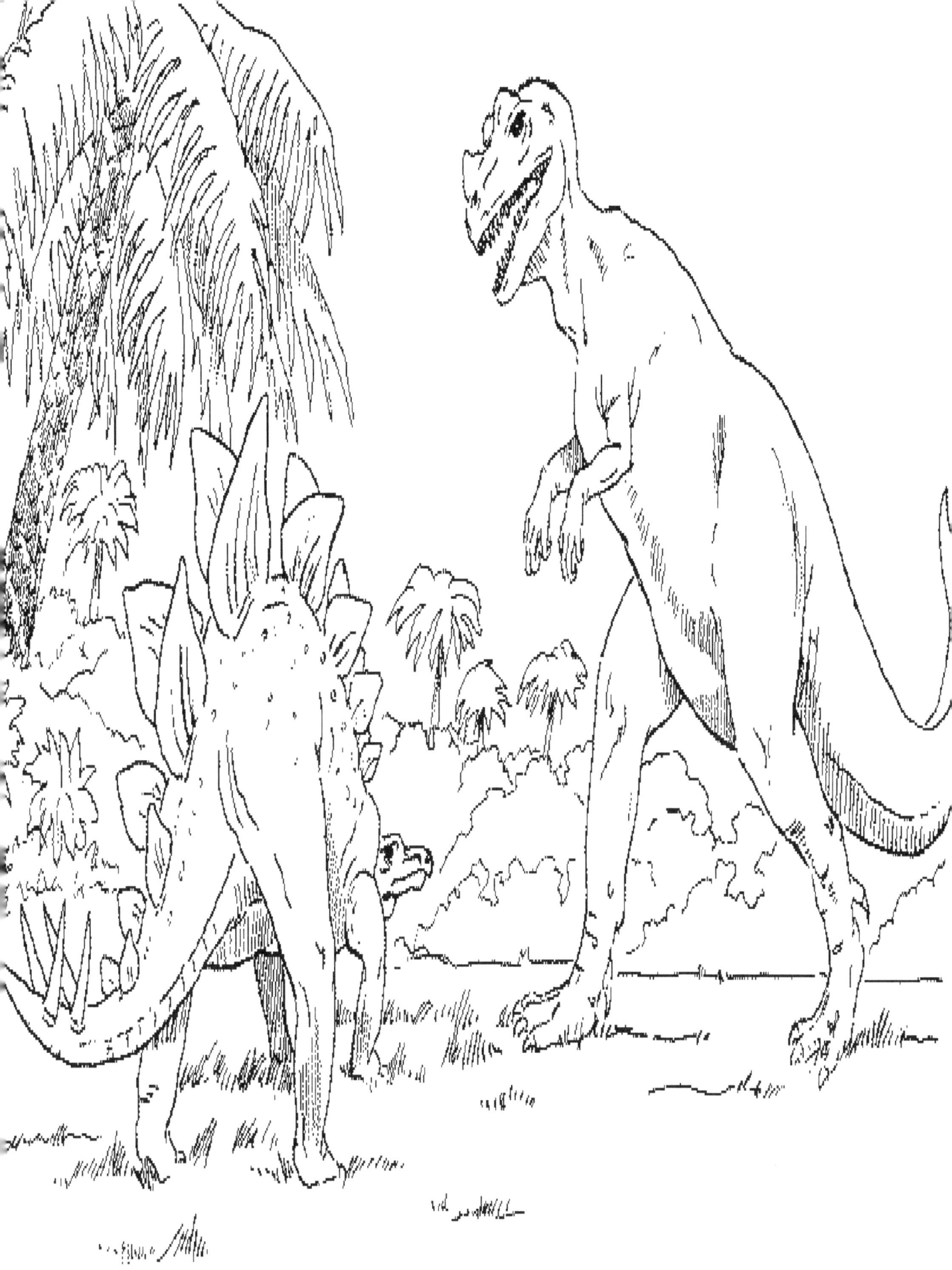

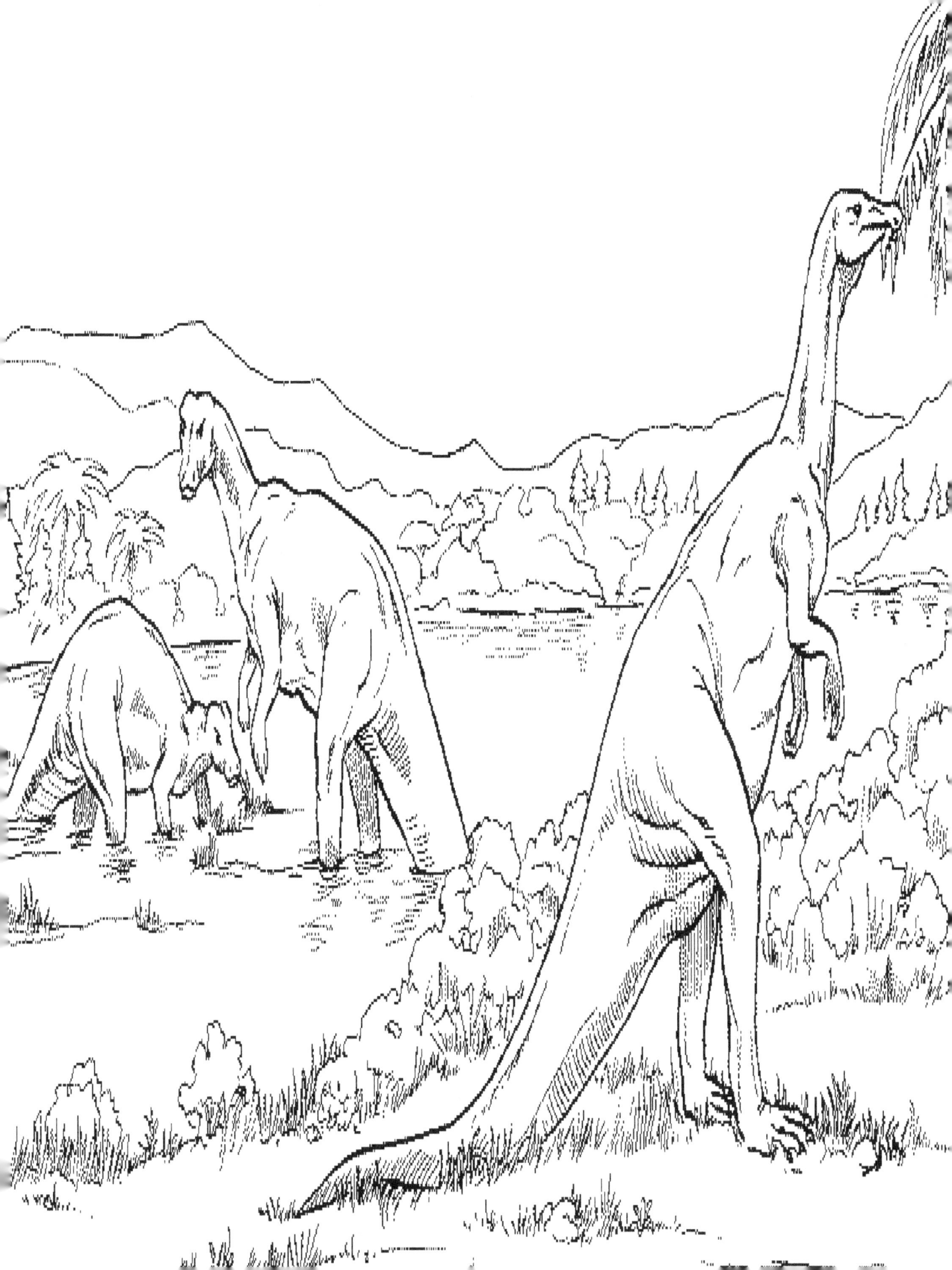

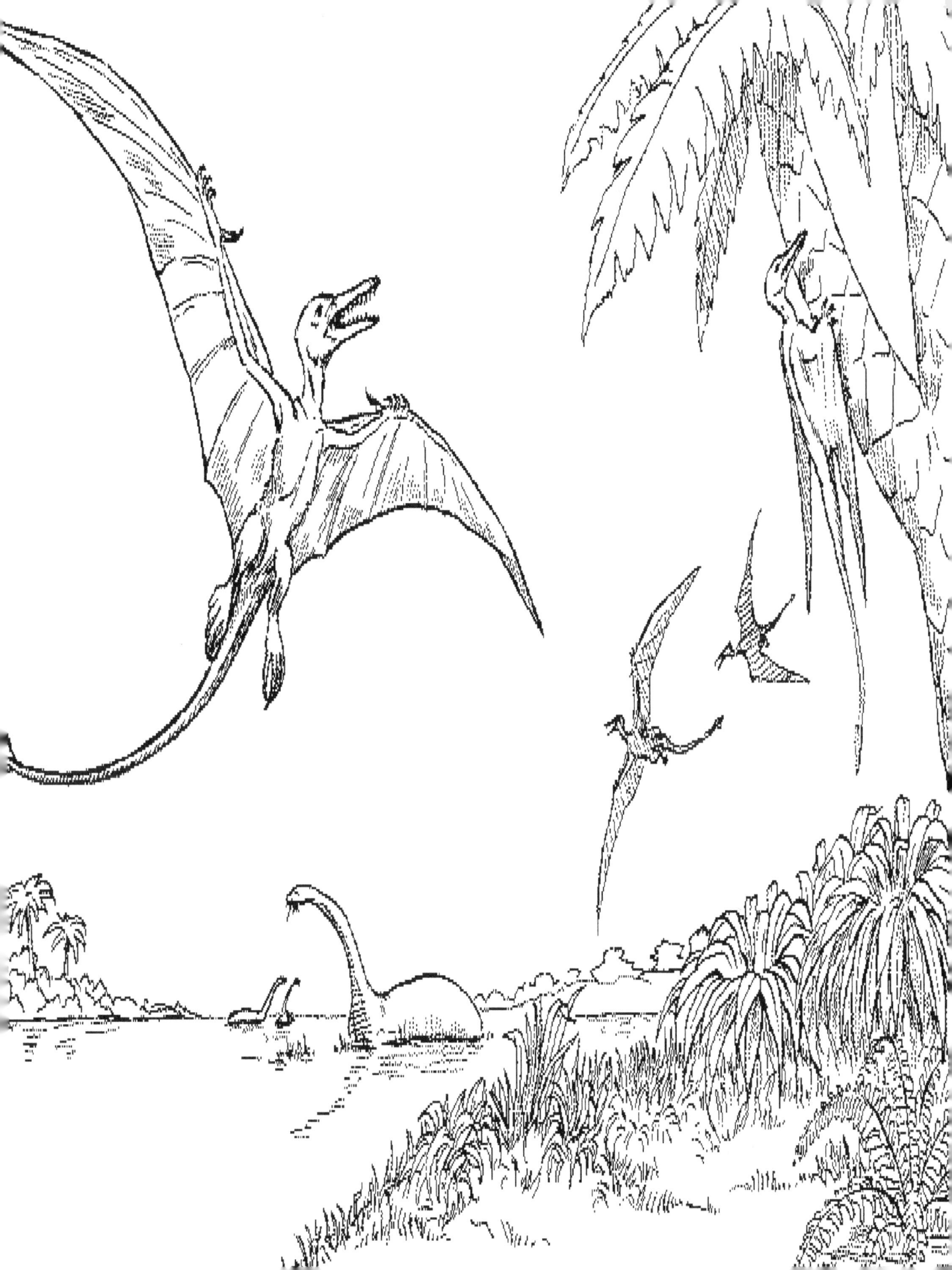

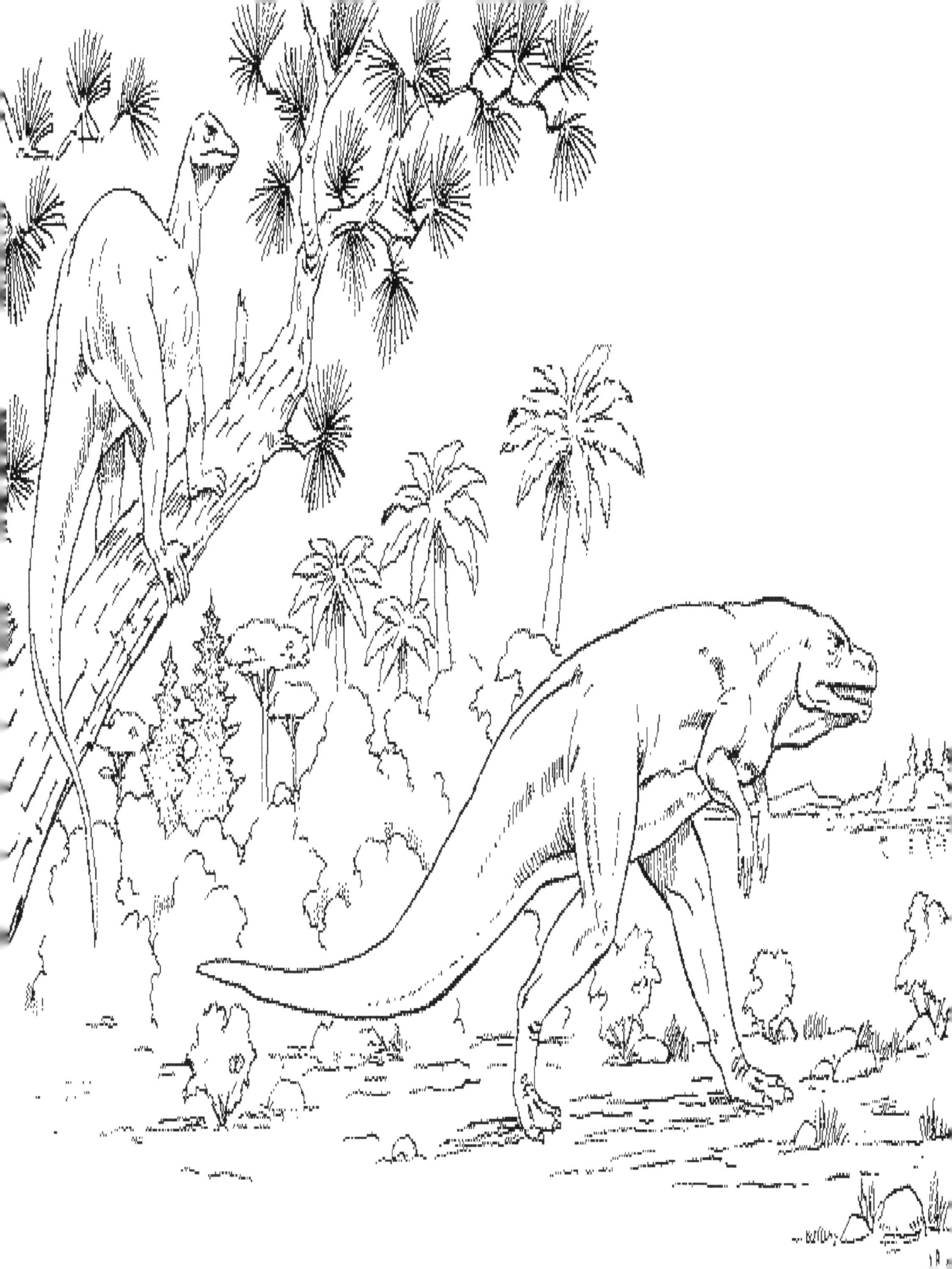

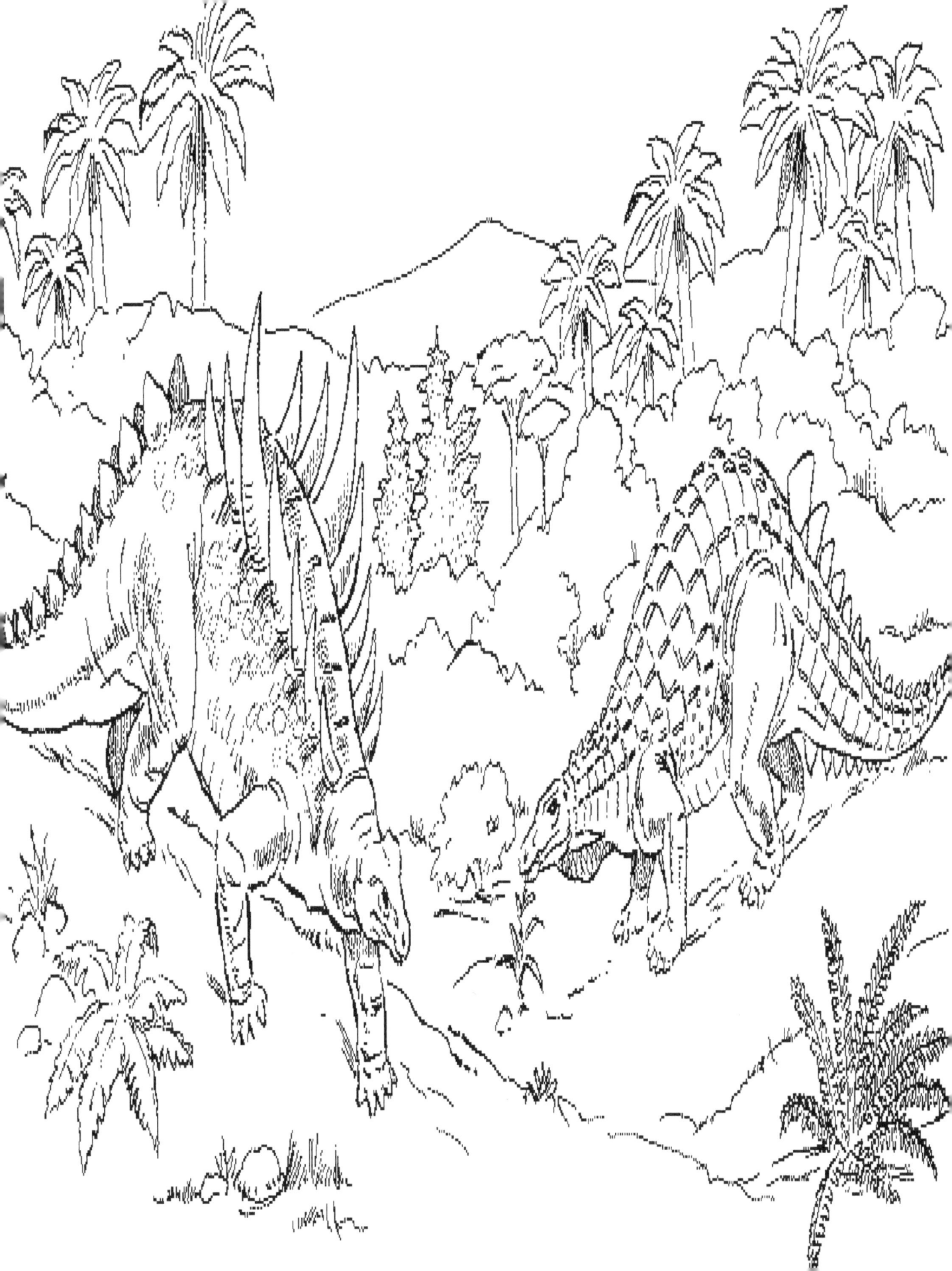

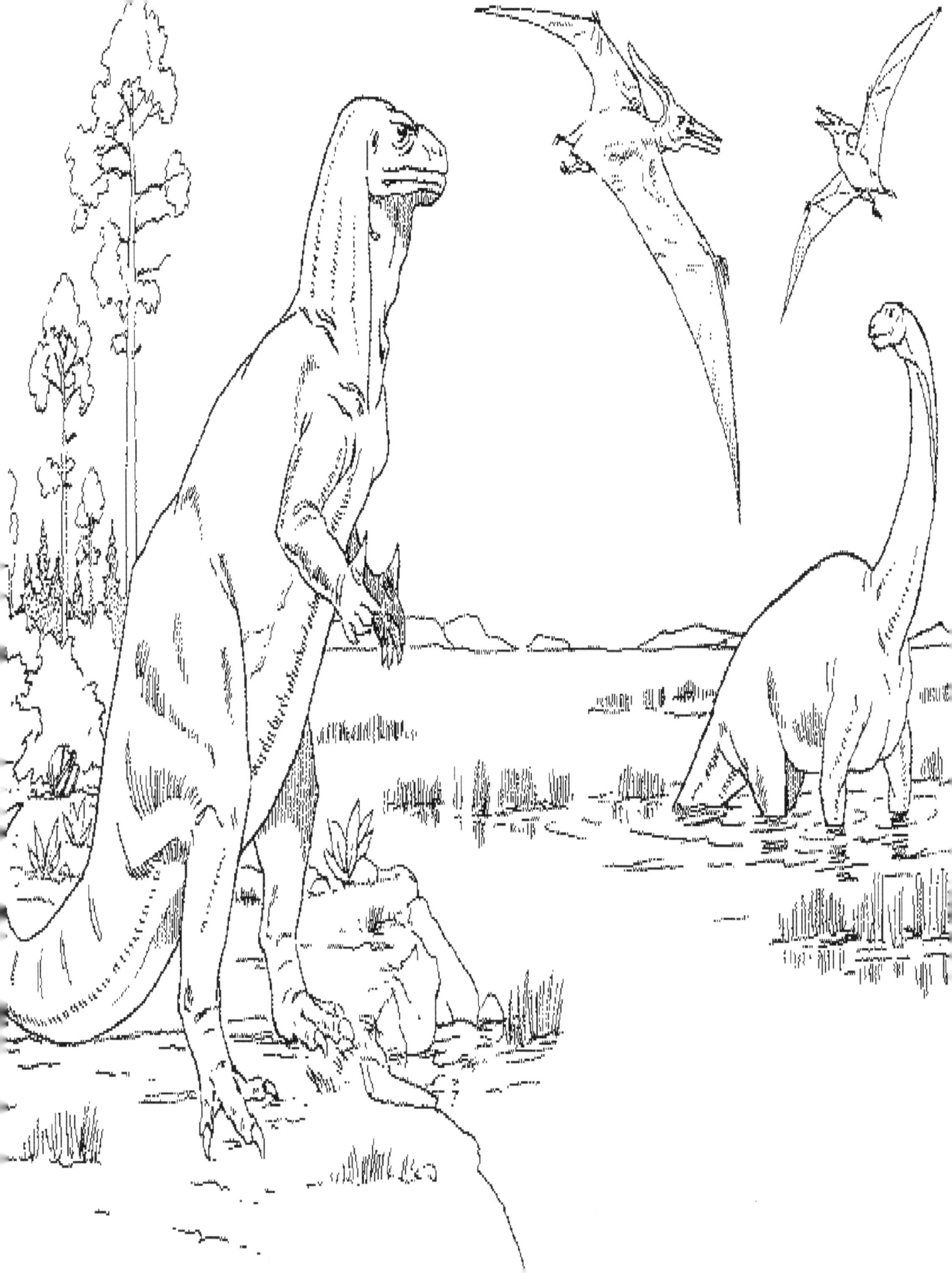

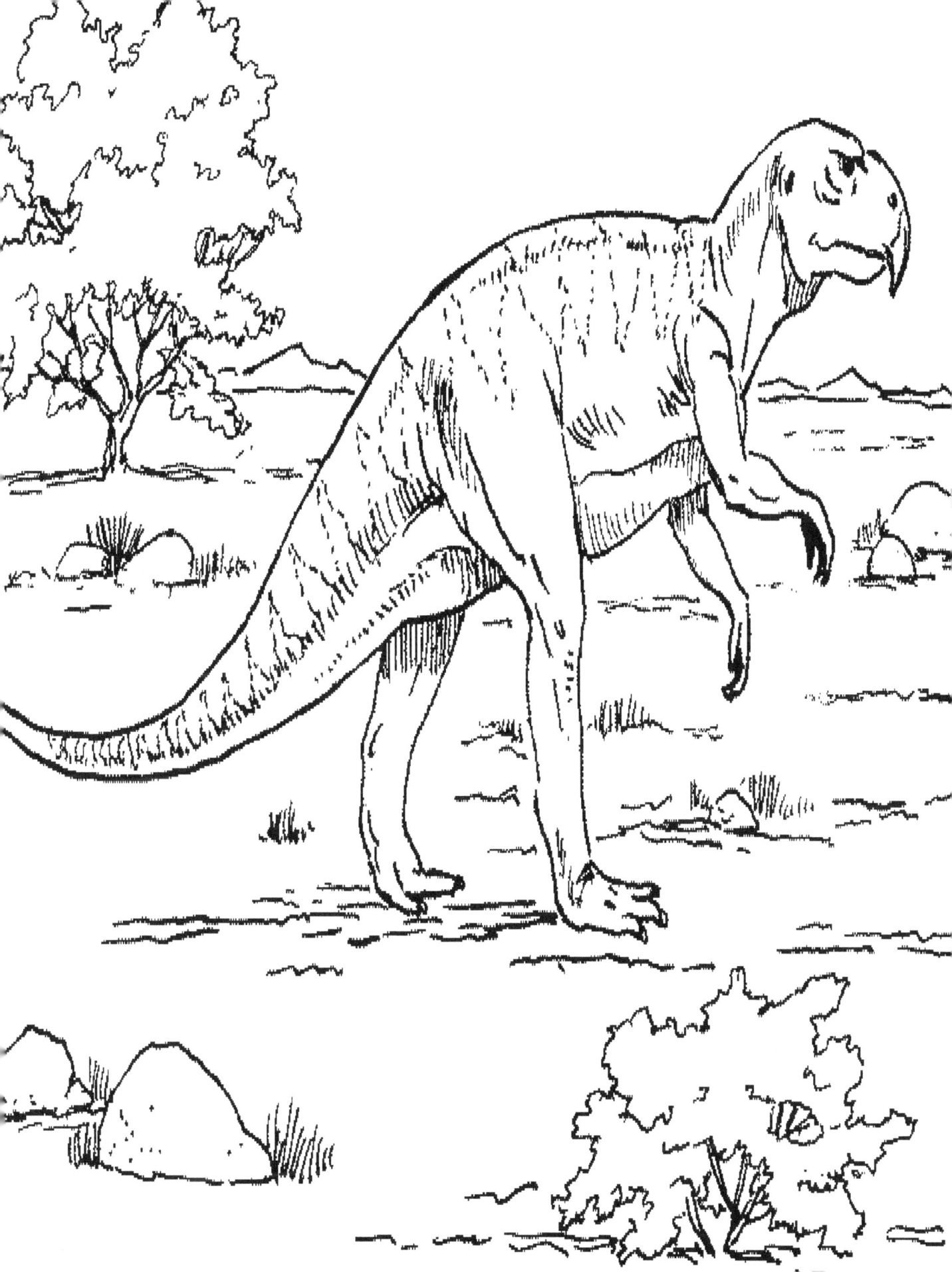

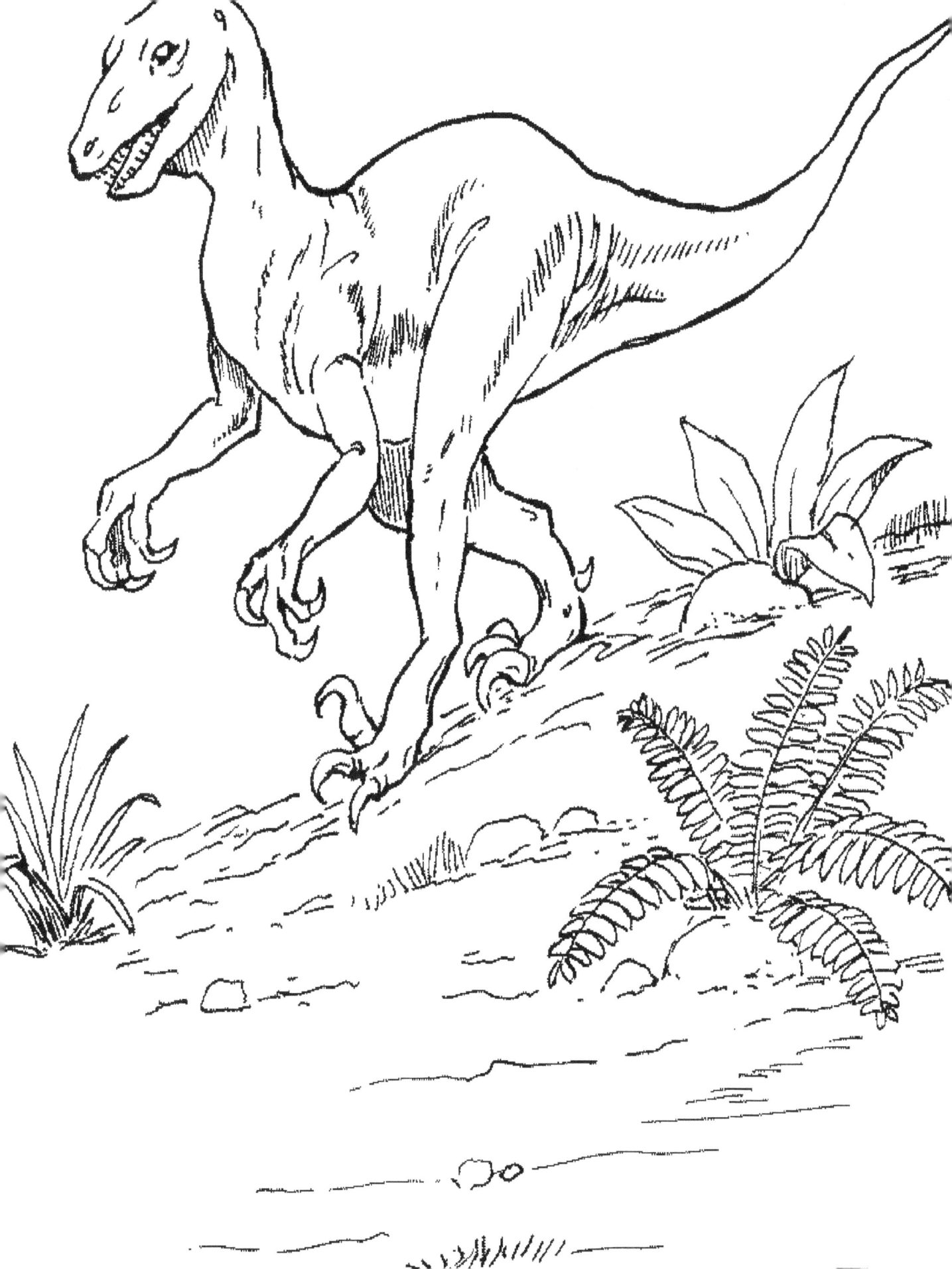

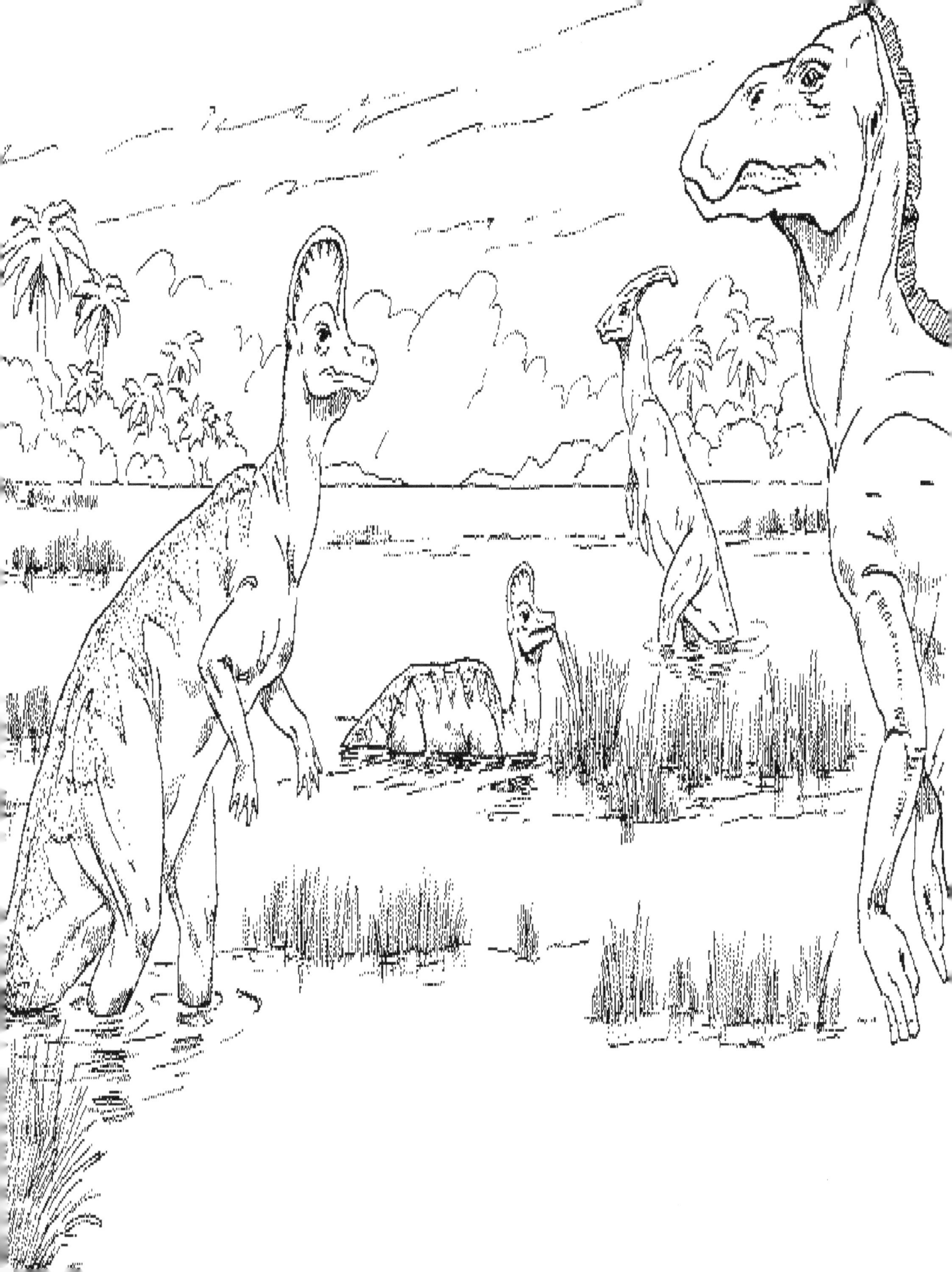

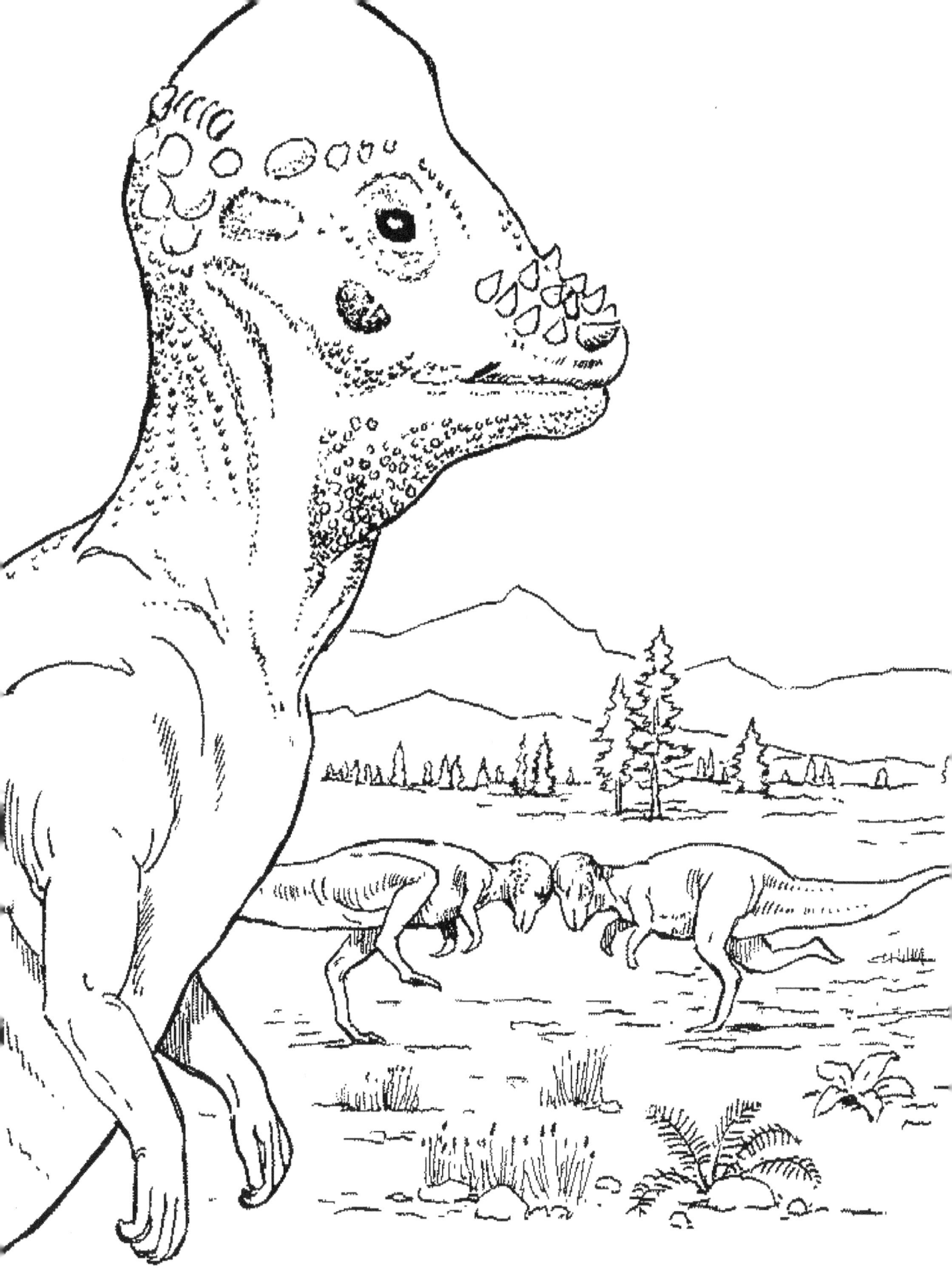

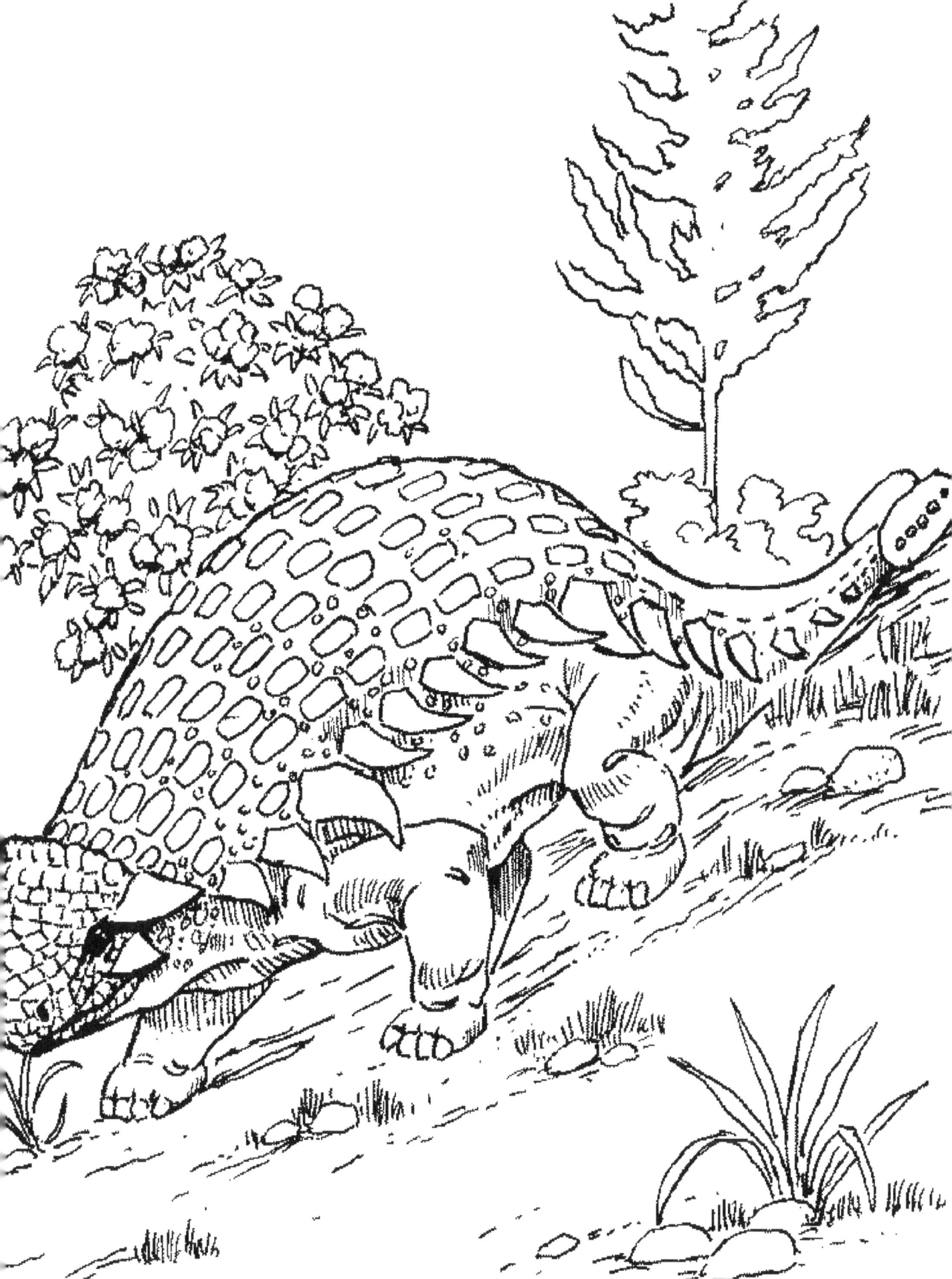

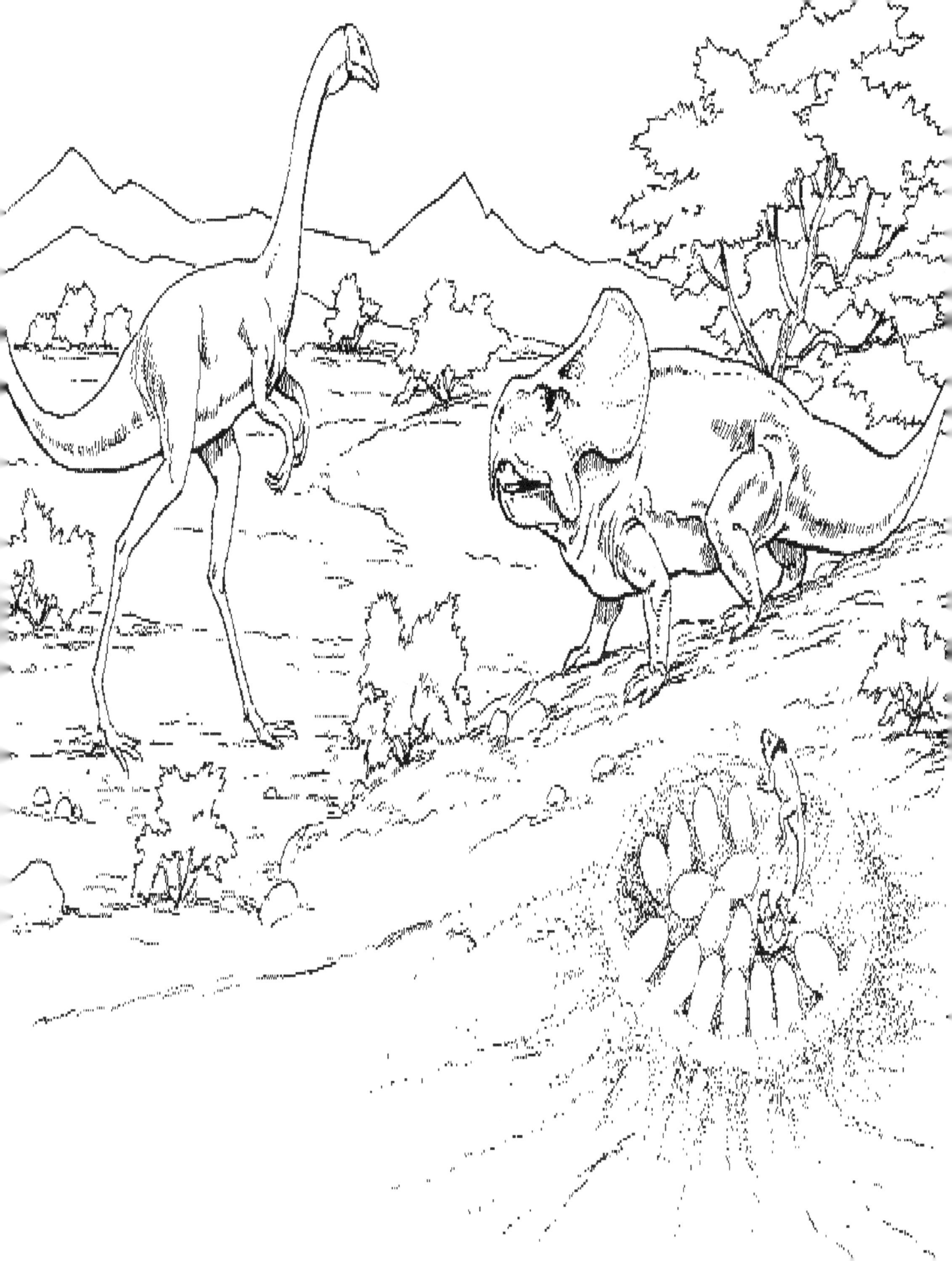

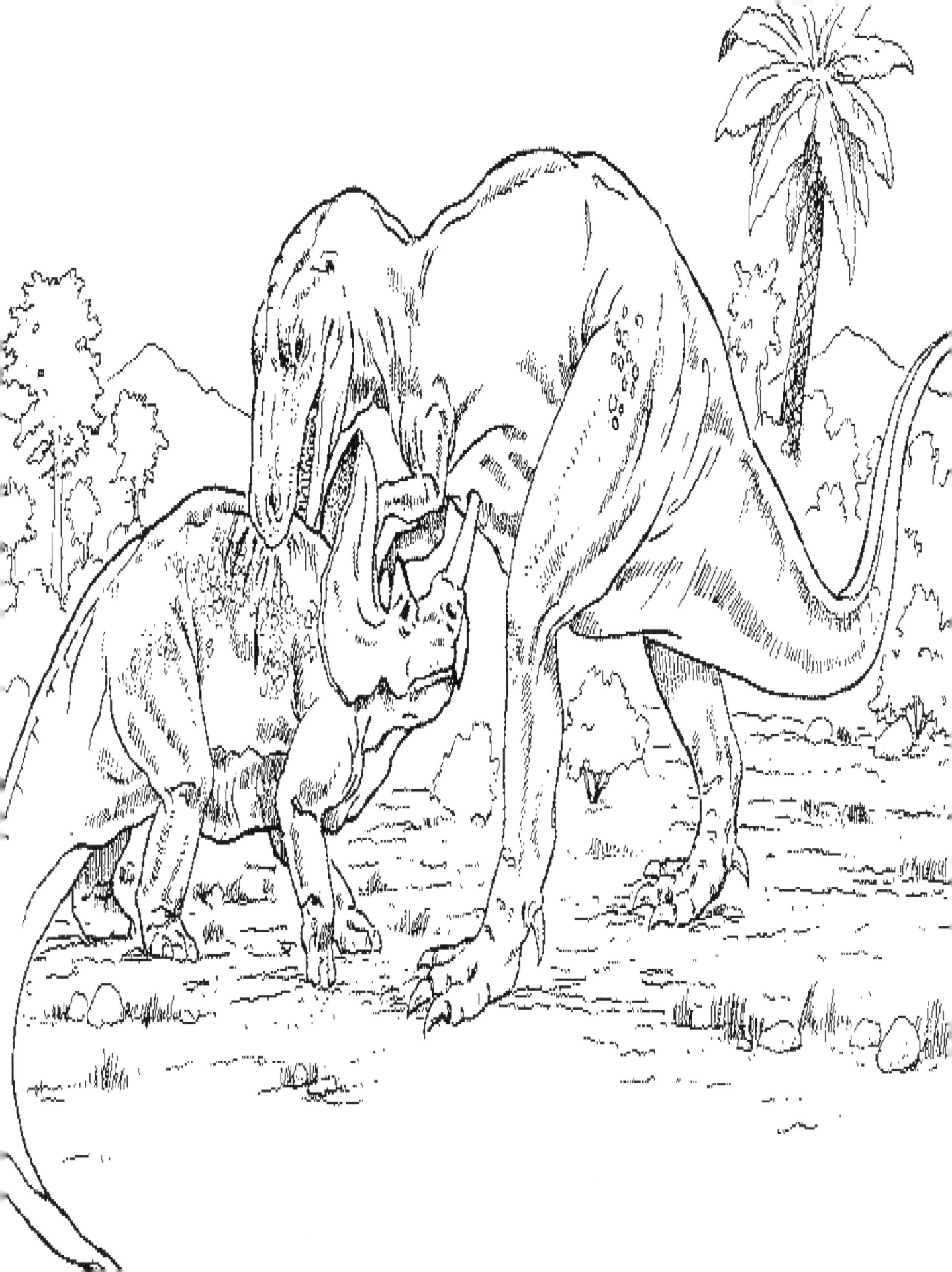

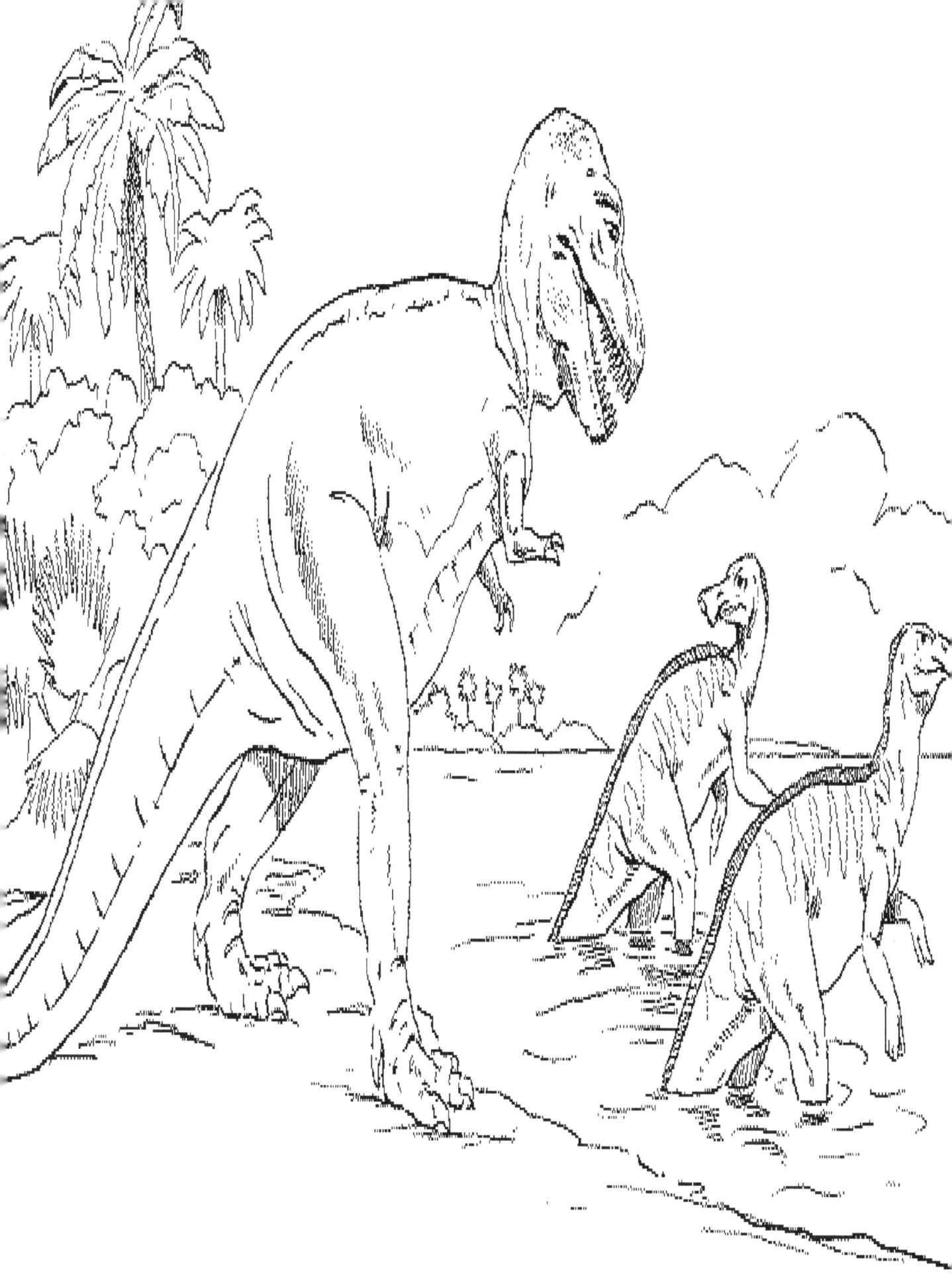

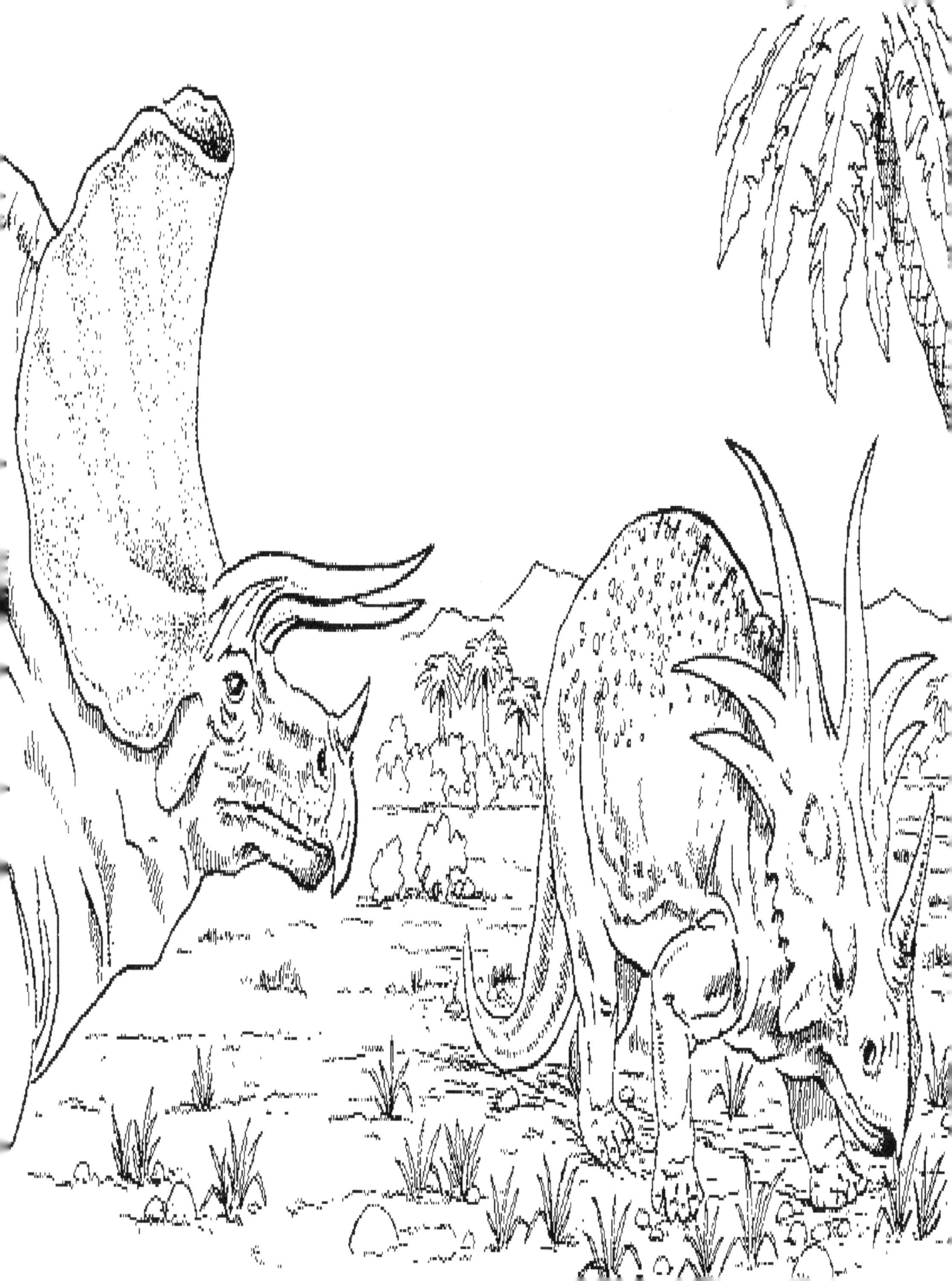

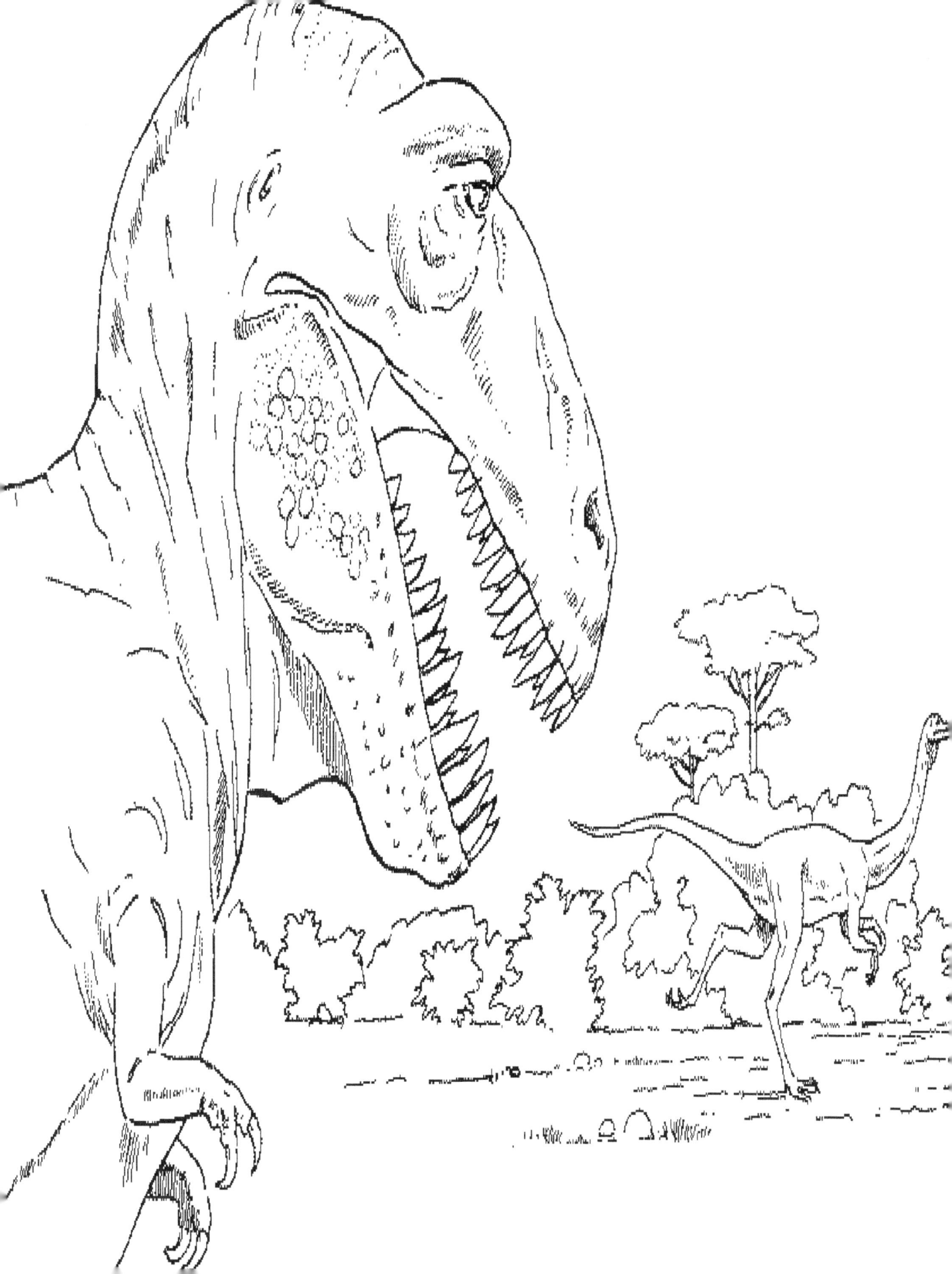

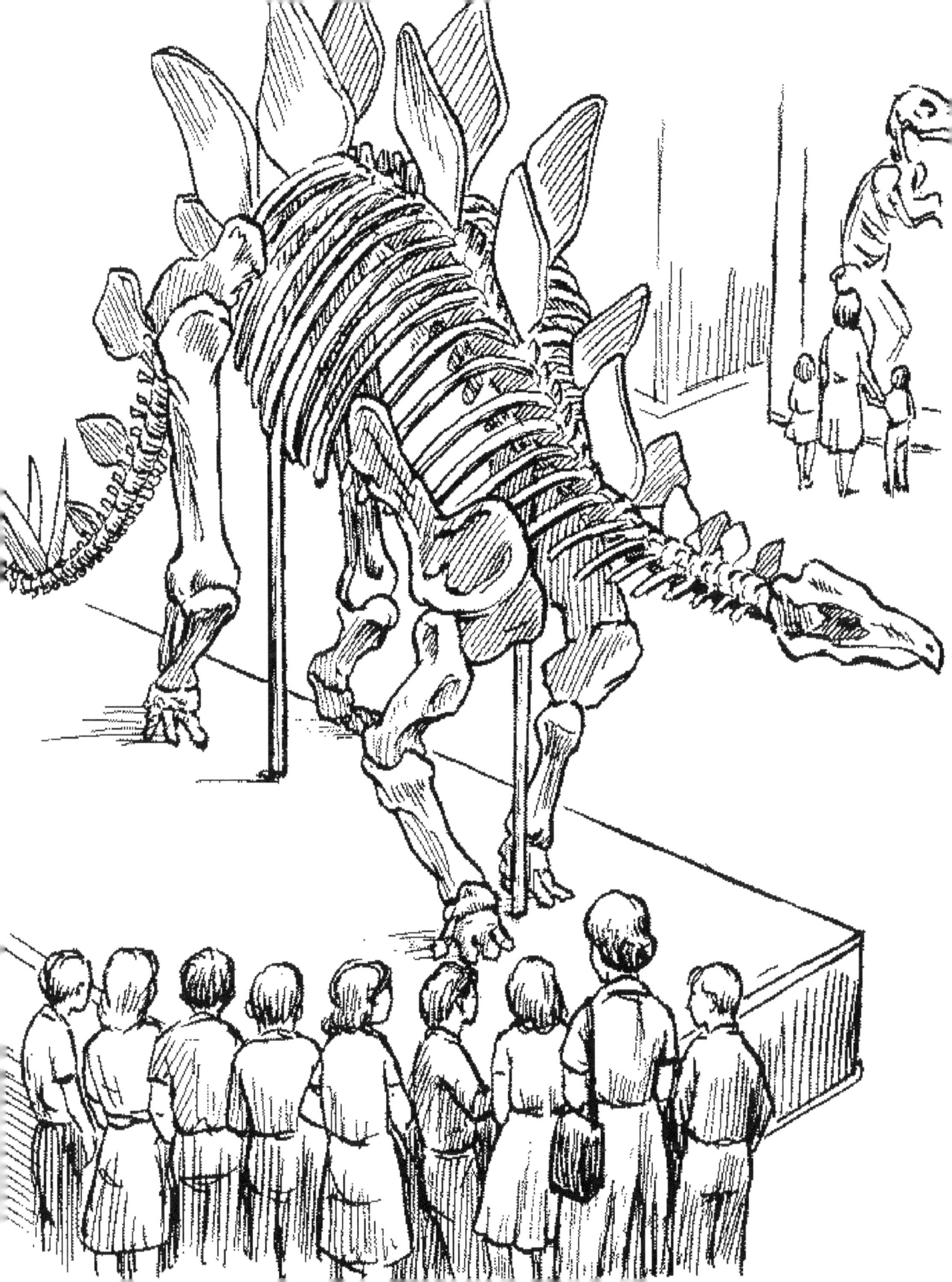

www.ingramcontent.com/pod-product-compliance
Lightning Source LLC
Chambersburg PA
CBHW081119280526
45787CB00007B/2900